Chalk Stories

Poems grounded in the landscape, history and people of Dorset

by
Beth Brooke

THE HOBNOB PRESS

2023

First published in the United Kingdom in 2023

by The Hobnob Press,
8 Lock Warehouse, Severn Road, Gloucester GL1 2GA
www.hobnobpress.co.uk

British Library Cataloguing in Publication Data
A catalogue record for this book is available from the British Library

ISBN 978-1-914407-59-8

Typeset in Adobe Garamond Pro 14/17 pt.
Typesetting and origination by John Chandler

In 2021 I read an article in the *Guardian* newspaper about the first geological map of Britain. I live in Dorset and volunteer at the Dorset Museum, which has an excellent geology exhibition and a fabulous collection of fossils. The story of the map transfixed me and the museum helped me understand more. I started to write about the place where I live - the places of chalk, the coast, the heath, the people who live here and who lived here before me. Chalk Stories is about what lies beneath our feet and how it shapes everything.

1 Chesil Beach

The moon is down
    Land me here in the dark
    when the sea lies like
an invitation
    I will know my way home
along the shingle bank
rich with stones of quartz
and chalcedony   harder than
steel   and more enduring
    I will heave my sea legs
up to the crest

of this Jurassic shore   until
my hand closes   around
a pebble that fits
        in the cupped hollow
of my hand

2 Tectonic Drift

We begin, like all beginnings, with an ending,
a heating of the air, a rising of water, a split,
a flood.

Pangaea, the mother of continents, drifts
north, patiently succumbs to the ripping
of herself.

I board the boat, sail the Red Sea,
am swallowed by the Suez Canal, disgorged
into the Mediterranean .

Pangaea opens, lets in the teeming
waves that we will call Atlantic;

under the water my home takes shape.

The Mesozoic is a holy trinity, God creating
the world, not in a week but through millennia
of rising and retreating seas,

sand dunes and salt flats, rivers braiding land,
a sinking mass of algae transformed by
the press of time and ready for

my own drift north: Southampton Docks,
decades of growing, shifting until I settle
on the side of a Jurassic hill.

There are stories to tell here, creatures
hidden in its layers, sharp-toothed
monsters that roar in dreams.

Landscape histories are exposed by weather,
narratives like curled ammonites held
in the damp hands of children

who bring them home, finger trace the
spiralling ridges, try to imagine a
hundred million years ago.

I walk the shingle beach, pick over
the stones exposed by storms,
look for words gifted by a more ancient sea.

3 The Scrying Mirror

The soil is thin, flint knaps
and chalk, stones
turned by the plough.

There are shadow stains
of skull and femur,
ribs greened by copper.

The mistress of the mirror
lies, flexed
in the shallow of her grave.

She looks,
looks, scrys
our future, her past,

divines the oak,
whether it will grow
crooked or straight.

The tree roots tangle
with the jaw bones of the dead,
until they open and sing.

Listen, hear them sing
to the gulls that
follow the plough

and the gulls drum
their feet in rhythm
with the jawbone song

so worms deep in the earth,
thinking that they hear
the hum and beat of rain,

crawl to the surface
and are eaten.

4 New Year's Day Walk to The Stone Circle

First morning of a new millennium,
we walk.
The sky is low to the ground,
wet and grey, it obscures everything.

We make our way to the place of the stones,
experience the thrill of their emergence
little by little,
out of the mist.

They stand in a circle, their backs to us,
backs to the world;

for centuries now they have had other business,
no longer interested in what we do.

We come to a halt, stand at the edge
await admittance.
Will they give it, open the gate between
this moment and the past?

My younger son, a single decade old,
steps forward, reaches out,
places his palm against the nearest stone,
begins to sing, and his song is ancient, wordless.

5 The Ridgeway Road

I
Before they finished
the new road
some wag put up a sign
saying
Welcome to the North,
which made me laugh;
there are pockets of north
in everything,
regardless of the compass.

II
When they cut the chalk

they found
a pit of burials,
heads on one side
separate from the rest
of them.
Fifty Viking men dug up,
Norsemen, Northmen,
men with north embedded
in their bones.

III
They called it a relief road;
incongruous, given
the numbers it funnelled into town.
Imagine a road as the cavalry,
driving over the ridge
to rescue us from the tyranny
of broad horizons.

IV
They made surgical cuts
in the chalk,
scars reminding everyone
that change happens,
even in geology.
The cuts healed, the banks
on either side began to show
the shift in seasons,

cowslip and kidney vetch -
unanticipated gifts;
the sun rose in the east
cast shadows
on the road.

V
In the spring and summer of
plague we stood on the ridge
to watch the cruise ships
anchored in the bay -
whales on the brink of beaching,
panic-stricken,
held between a shrinking
sea and sky, their north and
south always just out of reach,
compass needle spinning.

6 Chalk

I Map

Chalk ribs
curve from the north
    along the coast
        down to the Wash,
        cartographer renders
    a sinuous sweep of
        pale lime within a
        marbled mass of colour:
    pink for the Cambrian
of Wales, blue for the
        glistening, seething

swamps of the Carboniferous.
Lime white chalk,
     Cretaceous,
         when the world warmed
the seas rose.

II. Coccoliths

An abundance of
the microscopic,

coccoliths
in a warming ocean

birthed and bloomed,
died and drifted,

settled on the ocean floor,
quiet accretion of millennia.

III. Collision

Slow dance of tectonic plates,
bump and grid of the earth's mantle;
slow motion collisions lift,
twist ocean floor into land.

IV. South Dorset Downs

Hills roll, undulate:
wave form rendered
in soft rock.
Thin green skin
gashed in places,
exposing the white
bones beneath.

V. Swallet Hole

Rain shivers
through soil
finds the cracks, the
rock's capillaries;
chemistry does its work.
The ground sinks,
hollows itself.

VI. Winterbourne

Camel- hump hills
soak up winter rain
as if to keep at bay
the hard-earth hardship
of a dry summer.

Water swells,
bubbles,
sings out along tracks,
flows in roadside ditches;
unlikely riches of a winter season.

7 Some of us are made of this place

its archaeology seeps
through the soles of our feet
as we walk its banks and ditches.

This chalk has formed our bones and teeth,
our ancestors lie in its shallow
pit graves and weathered tumuli;
the soil is littered with their tokens
of knapped flint.

We thumb each piece,
feel the bulb of percussion, the
worked edges.
We salute the maker,
the unearthed stone a handshake
across millennia.

8 Learning The Bronze Age At Dorset Museum

Around five thousand years ago
new objects appeared-

bronze axe heads, archer's wrist guards
made of polished stone;

gold, embossed with patterns of
a fine geometry;

clay bowls decorated with
rope twist lines and sharp dots,

generous in their capacity to hold;
amber beads, bone pins, so many

things buried in the earth mounds
along the chalk ridge.

We know these people
who have gifted us

bone fragments in an urn,
a maker's thumb print on the pot.

9 Strontium Story

A thousand years from now they will open my mouth
and my bones will sing the story of my life,

how I was a traveller, a rider of sea and air
a walker of dunes, deserts and chalk downs;

they will take my teeth for analysis and find
strontium, learn the where and when of me,

will tell the way the sun shone, the richness
of the soil that grew the fruit my mother bought at
market.

Each layering isotope, like a tree-ring, marks my
growth
reveals the famine and the feast of what I was.

10 Seasonal Affective Disorder

It begins with the odour of dead roses,
late blooms of October caught off guard
by November frost.

Small sadnesses creep in:
        the shortening of days, slanting shadows,
the fading of meadows from green to straw beige.

Then there is grief
                    at the unleafing of beech trees,
their nakedness stark against an ash-washed sky.

There is misery as sodden paths
crust with ice that seems

            primed to crack and splinter
underfoot
            as we trudge

past cattle steaming in the morning cold.
They stare at us,
            dull-eyed, mournful.

Still, we walk
            press on,
stare up from time to time and scan
the empty sky.

11 Party Like It's The Cretaceous (2016)

I was itinerant once
but now   my dust has settled
in Jurassic Park

There are dinosaurs
which act   as though

the Romans
never happened

(bloody incomers)

party like it's
the Cretaceous
or at least 1956

(good times   good times)

mutter about the
availability of our British fish

12 Trouble In Hardy Country, April 2020

We are the pitchfork vigilantes,
See us seething down the lane,
looking for walkers to admonish,
looking for cyclists to shame.

It keeps us busy in pandemics,
it gives us stuff that we can shout,
We love when we find a walker,
it's something to get cross about.

We're really good at telling people
to go home and not come back.
We did it over immigration
when Brexiting was all the rage

so lockdown's been a Godsend really,
it's put us back on centre stage.

We had Union flags and UKIP banners
but pitchforks really are more fun,
they help us get you lot to
fuck off - literally a job well done.

So, we're the pitchfork vigilantes,
watch us seething down your lane,
looking for runners we can punish,
looking for someone we can blame.

13 My One Essential Journey Through The Town.

The silence of abandonment
drifts through the streets,

settles like dust on shop
window mannequins that pose

in breathable hiking jackets
and skis we no longer have a use for.

Instead we have the temerity
of birdsong; blue and apricot skies of

unbearable beauty; an invitation to
be still for long enough to remember

the things we had forgotten.

14 How it Was

We clothed our fear in
brightly coloured masks,
hid our smiles;
learned to hold our breaths

as strangers passed us
on pavements, stepped out
into the road to evade
the contagion of human touch.

However hard we scrubbed
we knew our hands
now never could be clean.

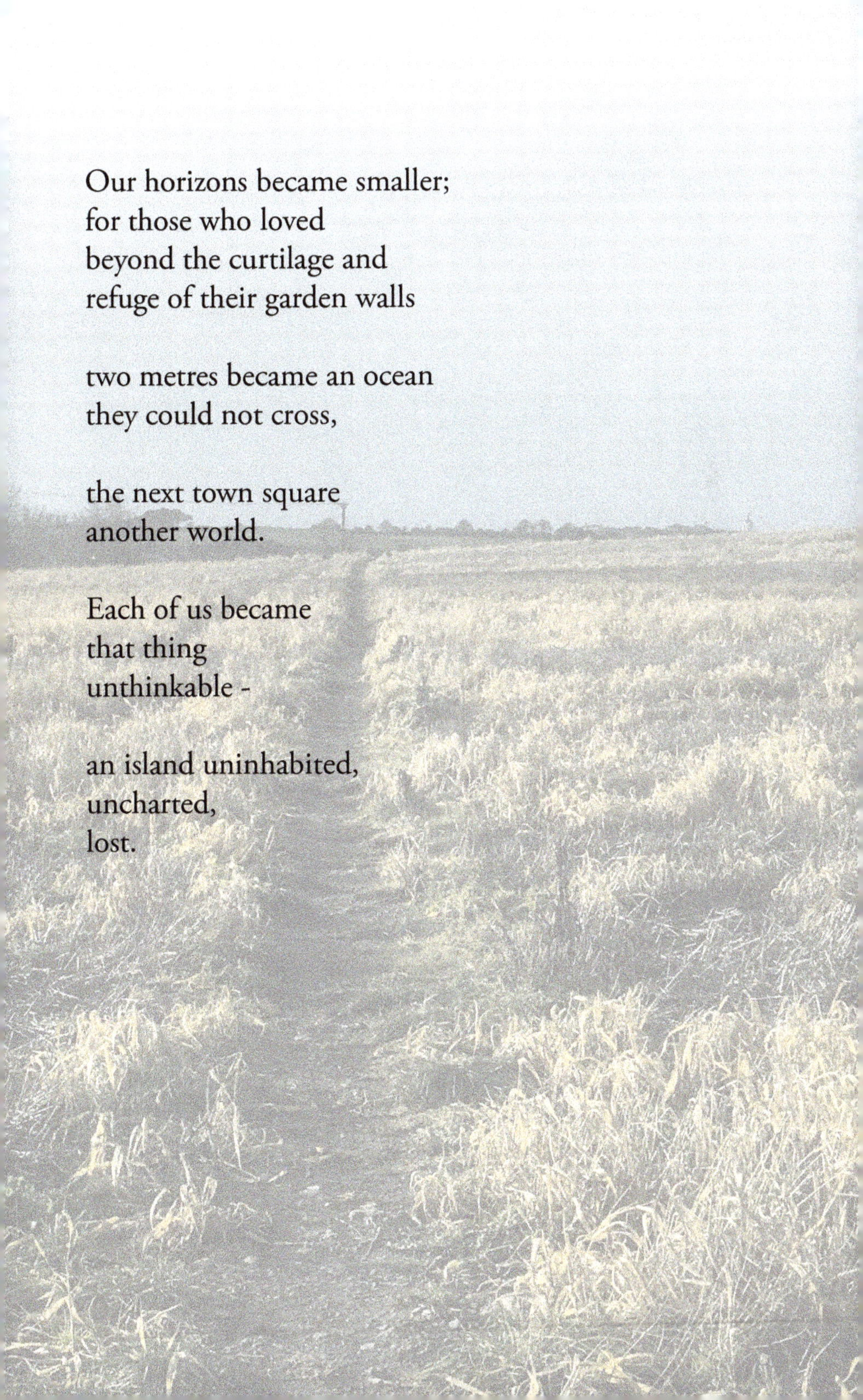

Our horizons became smaller;
for those who loved
beyond the curtilage and
refuge of their garden walls

two metres became an ocean
they could not cross,

the next town square
another world.

Each of us became
that thing
unthinkable -

an island uninhabited,
uncharted,
lost.

15 At Bridport Market

Hand-knitted men,
wicker-basket women
wander the marketplace,
pick over curios on the bric-a-brac stalls.

They exclaim in awe
at the witches bottle,
the mummified cat's paw,
wrapped in a faded velvet, stiff
with a century of chimney soot.

They thumb through books of spells
which fall open at the pages pertaining

to impotence and rage,
how to conjure
mindfulness from fury, all
interesting, but not the charms
these souls are looking for.

They rummage fruitlessly for
cures for unkind words,
balms to protect against deceit,
a potion which will pluck
honesty out of the mouths of liars.

16 Superheroes in Waitrose Car Park

Spider-man and his brother
wait by the car;
they have been shopping
with their mum.
They stand there as
she stows the groceries;
frustratingly, she doesn't seem
to need their help.
Spider-Man scans the car park
anyway,
looking for problems he could
fix with wall-climbing or
a bit of spider-silk.

Mum opens the car door,
the pair climb in;
the Spider- brother
gives me a thumbs up,
a sheepish grin
as if to say he knows
the lives of superheroes
aren't all the comics
make them out to be.

17 Pitch and Toss

Dost think because thou art virtuous,
there shall be no more cakes and ale?

Them stocks were a girt laugh,
Di'n't care what the Mayor said.
So what if the church were doin'
its divine office? Bain't a problem
for us 'cos we weren't goin'.
Upright citizens, he said,
were complainin' 'bout the noise.
We were only playin' pitch 'n' toss,
the Burt brothers had a whole
shillin' between 'em an' George

an' me were lookin to win it.
Reckon we wud've too if the
constable hadn't carted us off.
Three hours in the stocks we got,
you'd think we were a circus
act the way the whole of Mill Street
flocked to see us.
Made us famous though,
'specially when I told 'em I wud've shown 'em
my divine office but t' stocks meant
I were sat on it.

*In April 1843 six young men, some described as boys
were placed in the stocks outside Fordington Church
for three hours. The punishment assigned by the Mayor
was because they had played pitch and toss outside the
church while the Divine Office (Sunday service) took
place. They were noisy, someone complained. They were
not contrite!*

18 Van Amburgh's Elephant Bathes in the Sea

Van Amburgh's menagerie claimed royal
appointment;
its presence in the seaside town a sensation;
even the mid-summer sky was dressed
in its blue and gauzy Sunday best to mark the arrival
of Mr Van Amburgh's Royal Collection.

From the King's Statue to the turnpike gate,
Weymouth's pavements heaved with people,
how they had longed for such a spectacle.

Those that could afford the fare and possessed
a spirit of adventure, climbed the elephant's

embellished howdah,
rode and swayed upon its back,
penny maharajas.

Later, the creature was made to parade
along the Weymouth esplanade.

People cried in wonder at it,
gasped at every aspect of the thing,
its greyness, its fissured oak-bark skin,
the preposterous nature of its fly-whisk tail,
that nose so long, so unlike anything.

Who knows if any were unsettled by
those long-lashed and rheumy eyes?
To the people who followed to the water's edge
its quietness was as ferocious as lions,
its self-containment far more threatening.

On the beach the elephant fanned its ears,
swayed its head,
greeted the sea,
explored the pebbles offered by waves,
anointed itself.

Buoyed up by water,
the day's indignities drifted away:
the elephant became itself again.
It played: its trunk a hose, a periscope.

Then tents packed, lions caged,
the elephant, too large, too much
to be enclosed came out of the sea,
walked the roads to the next town,
the next excited crowd.

Frolicsome, the newspaper said
and those who saw would not forget.
Did the elephant, like those who watched,
commit to memory,
its fifteen glorious minutes in the sea?

*In June 1842 Mr Van Amburgh's 'Royal Collection' of
animals made a tour of Dorset. On 16th June 1842,
the Dorset County Chronicle reported on the visit to
Weymouth including the elephant sea bathing. Unlike
the other animals, the elephant had to walk from one
town to the next.*

19 Lion Taming

Gasps, groans,
moaning breaths,
fill the tent with anticipation.
Shillings paid, the audience
waits for the thrill.

The lions circle
the bars of the cage,
snarl resentment
at the shadows,
and at the Maestro, ready
to make his entrance.

Lions and people roar,
the Maestro bows,
acknowledges
the acclamation.
He cracks his whip
and then
steps lightly into
the lions' den.

Crowd and lions tremble;
they are in awe.
The Maestro lays hold
of the nearest lion,
seizes it by the jaw,
forces it, by his strength
of will, into a hot, red,
gaping maw.

The crowd erupts
at such a scene:
the king of beasts
so subjugated,
mild, as any English beast
that grazed their fields,
pulled their ploughs,
or took an apple
from fond hands.

In 1842, Mr Van Amburgh brought his menagerie to Dorchester and Weymouth. The Dorset County Chronicle reported on his lion taming act.

20 William Barnes: polymath, poet, wearer of shoes

Look!

These are a poet's shoes,
a pastor's shoes, the shoes
of a man who learned to
praise the god of nature
in a dozen languages.

Low-heeled, square-toed,
still with a hint of polish,
they whisper good sense
and faith in the power
of words.

These are shoes
that stood in drawing rooms
pulpits, and school rooms,
walked the miles between
parishioners, the weddings,
baptisms and funerals that
formed the last and leather of their lives.

These are a poet's shoes,
look at their buckles.
Gilded leaves and forget-me-nots
hint at lyricism,
the wearer's gift of tongues.

Calf-skin lining holds
the imprint of his feet,
place your hand inside,
feel the gait and rhythm of
his poet's stride
over chalk hills,
and water meadows,
down rutted lanes.

These are the shoes that
walked in darkness, knew
the light. These aren't just
anyone's shoes, these are
the shoes of William Barnes,
polymath, pastor, poet.

21 Her Hanging

Harsh words, hard hands,
another whipping.

No justice for a wife
more than a dog.

She wields the axe
against his years of lashing,
a cur's bite,
bared teeth provoked
into piercing flesh.

Cruelty is no mitigation
where justice is concerned,

a man dead is
murder, however loud
scars on a woman's back
plead attention.

The day of reckoning
becomes a holiday
in the old tradition -
a hanging fair: villages
empty their citizens
into the town
for a beer, a pie,
a game of skittles, and
the hanging of Elizabeth
Martha Brown.

Close to the scaffold
Dorset's future famous son
notes her figure, shapely
in the black silk dress
that whispers as she moves
towards the ceremony
of her pinioning,
sees how the muslin cloth,
intended to obscure
her face, becomes
transparent in the rain.

After the drop,
he watches the body
wheel half round
and back upon the rope;
he thinks
how beautiful it is.

The crowds disperse,
the taverns fill.
Fiddles strike up.
There will be dancing later.

In August 1856, Elizabeth Martha Brown was
publicly hanged outside Dorchester prison for the
murder of her husband. She had often suffered
violence at his hands. Thomas Hardy, aged sixteen,
attended this event which was accompanied by
a 'hanging fair', an opportunity for people to
enjoy a holiday. About thousand people witnessed
this execution. In old age Hardy admitted he felt
ashamed that he had gone to the hanging. He drew
upon it when writing *Tess of the D'Urbervilles.*

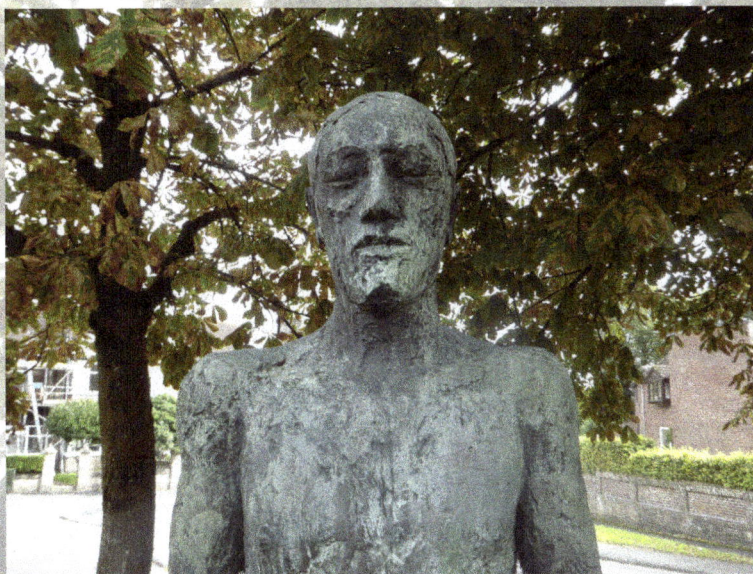

22 The Child Arsonist

He dreams of fire.
In his imagination hears
the crackling hiss and
rhythm of it;
it makes him want
to dance.

He waits for the judge
to pass the sentence,
pronounce his doom,
watches how the courtroom
crowd leans in,
eyes wide, mouths open,

eager for the words that
come with the donning
of a black cloth.

He thinks how cold it was
in February, how bleak,
how black the sky; nothing
to warm the heart or
heat the edges of him,
wonders why they
did it, thinks of the
beauty of the flames.

He knows why John and Davey
blamed it all on him, hoping
to save themselves from
a length of Bridport rope,
but how they had laughed
when the hemp bales burned
and sparked the thatch;
they jigged and waltzed
at that.
Judgement is given,
the punishment harsh;
he is led by the guard to
the cells and the dark
of the underground, the
shadow world of waiting
for whatever mercy

might be given to a boy
who danced with flames.

The hangman favours
the short drop,
believes that life
is best squeezed out
of the guilty,
likes to see his
clients dance upon
the rope, each jerking
step upon the air
a victory for justice.

The boy is slight,
the prison governor
brings the mercy that
he can: two leads weights
bound to each of the prisoner's
skinny legs;
the governor thinks,
this boy is done with dancing.

** Silvester Wilkins aged 15, was sentenced at the
Dorchester Assizes in 1834 to death by hanging. His
crime was arson. The jury asked for mercy but the
judge decided that hanging was a better option. There
are examples of mercy weights in the Dorset Museum.*

23 Dorset Museum At Night

At night   after the doors close
   the museum is left to itself

     Artefacts murmur
shift in their cases

In the gallery dedicated to
a famous author are a child's shoes

If we could open their cabinet
it would reek

    of hand-me-down lives
    hardship

These shoes are treasures

  there is poignancy in the worn heels
broken stitching   patched soles

In the next room
    is an emerald silk dress
    a bride's trousseau

It twirls on its stand   glitters
under the spotlights
    an emblem of a post-war hope
    promise   of a brighter   freer world

24 The Woodpecker Sends Out A Message

This
        is the utter winter of a field
                starve-acre of chalk and flint in
equal measure.

There are brown and yellow tattered shoots,
        straggled lines that came too late,
sprouted after the harvest cut
full of misplaced hope,
an irrational faith in September's
continuing warmth.

The footpath across is bare,
        compacted by the trudge of feet
determined
to walk into Spring and
its green stems of wheat.

From the stand of trees
on the southern edge
        a woodpecker
        taps out a fanfare for
the approaching equinox.

25 Birch Trees Sing In Puddletown Woods

We are the first, the new beginning,
ten thousand green hearts
raised towards the sky.

We are wind borne,
seed-small whispers laid upon the earth
to root in the heath and heather,
soften the hard edges.

Our grace is upright, white, dressed in
the transparency of moonlight, a beacon
to bring you from the frontier of night,
the long darkness of death.

The male and the female of us
bloom on the same bough,
we are the new beginnings,
green hearts raised up to the sky.
Look for us in the edge places,
in the damask rose of sunset
and the morning's bright.

26 A Communion With Nature

To the woods, they say, these sons of mine,
aged nine and seven.
We have been before, once
even at night to walk in darkness
with only the moon and the thrill of
our beating hearts for company.
Sometimes I am tempted to give them a
breadcrumb trail, but I think they know
the way home though if it should happen
that they did not and got distracted,
birds might eat the bread.
My heart…my heart at the thought of it.

The pits, they shout and set off running.
It is a ritual they have, communing not so much
with nature as with the spirits of young men
who scrambled up steep sided trenches into war.
They race each other up the slopes,

I scramble and they haul me up the final yards.
Oh, the wild laughter.
My heart…my heart at the sound of it.
The thread of molecules between us
pulls me after their young legs, the beauty of
knees marked by dirt and algae.

There is a fallen beech tree,
a swallet hole casualty.
The earth between its roots is useful
weaponry, clumps hard as metal;
it is for these they have come.
Chalk and clay grenades are flung
at tree trunk targets, or at the boulder
we are always surprised to find there,
standing sentinel between the heathland
and the wood.
The plosive sound of shattering earth
as the mark is hit matched by the huff and
whoop of their delight. They dance.
The wild laughter.
My heart…my heart at the sight of it.

27 On Worgret Heath

The air is liquid,
cool as river balsam.
Clear as still water,
the daylight
is deep enough
to dive into.

We walk beneath
this Indian summer sky,
breathe in
pine scented heath,
take time
to stand and look.

From within the curtilage
of the army ranges
comes the sound
of heavy guns; the
crump of artillery,
and spiteful chorus
of small arms' fire
vibrate across the fields.

The noise of it
roils through,
thumps
against our chests,
presses itself
against our heads
and out of nowhere
I find myself thinking,
'My God, -Aleppo.'

28 Today there is a cease-fire

The day offers itself- a gift -
wrapped in translucent silk
paler than a blackbird's egg;

mine to open.

Inside is the first
hour of all the mornings
there have ever been,

sunrise that tingles with
lemon-sharpness,

paper silhouettes
of trees against
the apricot wash
of a dawn horizon;

there is the cry of jackdaws,
the growl of pebbles
on the shoreline;

there is the silence that comes
after the guns stop firing.

29 Night Scape

The sound of tank fire from Bovington
Heath invades my sleep;
I lie and listen to the music
of a Dorset night:

the rumbling bow wave of
the midnight train that
ploughs the line to London;

the owl's first call
from the churchyard sycamore.
I wait, alert for the response.

St. Peter's bell rings the night office.
The cat pads in.

30 Crows on Eggardon Hill Fort

fling themselves at the wind,
bodyboarders launching
against incoming waves;

squawk with delight as
the air buffets them, hauls
them back, and they wheel,
tumble above
the ramparts, surf
the gusting breeze
with raucous glee -
again, again, again.

31 Nothing Was Happening

at least it seemed that way-
the usual sheep in the field, us
on the usual track to Bushes Barn,
and a sky that threatened rain;

a buzzard mewled in the overhead grey,
spiralled round and around,
with the usual crows mobbing and at last
the falling of the threatened rain,

which was at least something -
a jolt of energy into an otherwise

nondescript day - stair-rod rain
that stung our faces, sent us laughing,

stumbling over grassy hummocks
to the old barn, its huge doors
gone and roof tiles missing, but dry.
We had a moment to catch breath,

admire the glow of yellow gorse
against the rain-soaked sky and then
unexpectedly there was something,
something

that flew on silent wings, blinked its
black eyes in a pale dish face -
and this was the moment we had
waited for.

32 Walk To Clavell's Tower

Sky the colour of knapped flint;
rain falls with a sting that takes
the breath away, makes cheeks raw.
We hunch our shoulders,
dip our heads
against the weather and walk
to Clavell's Tower.

We climb the steep cut path,
punched by the wind, reach
the tower's honey-coloured walls,
stand on the cliff top, our backs
to this folly of privilege, lean
out just far enough to understand
the anger of the sea below us.

33 Rooks Return To The Town Walks

November, but it's sixteen degrees Celsius
and the rooks have returned, are massing
in the bare-leafed chestnut trees for whom
autumn came early because of the summer
heatwave and a three month drought.
The birds are cacophonous, and although
there's not so much as a breath of wind
the bare-branched canopies sway with the
force of these rookish gatherings.
I cannot speak rook but want to tell them
to go away, they are a full four months
too early and the trees, I suspect, are dead.

34 Sea Swim At Ringstead

The promise of cool salt sting
as we undress.
Shingle underfoot,

I hobble to the water's edge,
inch forward painfully
until the wave wash pulls
the pebbles under me
and I stumble.

The shock of it.

The water up, up,
over ankles, calves
knees, clenched thighs,

up, up, over groin, waist
until there is nothing for it
but to fling myself forward
into its breath-stopping
embrace.

35 Drought Comes To Langton Herring

We sit in bleached fields, the sun
has turned the ground into
a smashed pot, terracotta pieces
as far as the eye can see.

Everything is desiccated;
we are husks, brittle-skinned,
a rub of the hands reduces us
to dust.

Weeks pass, some of us burn,
dried by lack of rain, ignited by
relentless light and pounding heat.

In the far north, the ice melts.
Soon we will drown.

36 Under The Weather

Remember when it rained so much
it felt as though the sky
had spent itself with weeping;
flung itself, exhausted,
in sodden heaps across the fields?

It felt as if the very possibility of morning
hung balanced between our outward
and our inward breaths.

The weather asked a question we could not
answer and the day became fog, the air
tasting like ash in our mouths.

37 Travelling Home From Home

We drive to the station, your rucksack crammed
with treasures of the season - books, the obligatory
festive socks, artisan gin, and another of
those complicated games you help us navigate.

We embrace, promise to see each other soon
then you are gone, on the thirteen twenty-five
to Bristol Temple Meads and I go home to
a sad coffee, consolatory chocolate.

I need to rearrange myself into something in
keeping

with this newly reduced state: the small kingdom
of home has lost citizens today.

So, I make an inventory of groceries we need
tomorrow;
wash and clear the debris from the pre-departure
brunch.
I avoid climbing the stairs, will leave the sheets on
your bed
for a day or two so I can pretend for a while longer
you are still here.

38 Odyssey

I walk the darker hours down
the rain-washed pavements
of empty streets until I reach
what used to be my mother's house.

I stand at the gate.

Light leaks
through a curtained window;
whoever lives here now
is also restless: one of the old,
the lost, the dead,
who almost never sleep;
we wander endlessly,
ghosts in our own histories,
journeying home.

39 It's Winter Now

Today was a day of proper winter:
crunch stiff grass,
ice in rutted paths that
splintered under boots.
The sky was the colour of
a starling's egg and the sheep
in the lower field gathered
by the gate, waiting for the
farmer to bring hay.
You would have loved it.

40 Wasted Opportunities
after Thomas Hardy

You did not walk with me
and so you missed
the way the light played on the water,
the hiss and grunt of pebbles
as the waves rolled them ashore.

You did not stand with me
at the crest of the hill to watch
the sunset change the sky
into an upturned bowl of peach
and raspberry.

You did not come with me to watch
the kingfisher's vibrant thread of
blue and orange pierce the surface
of the river to catch the silvered fish.

Your loss, I think.

www.ingramcontent.com/pod-product-compliance
Lightning Source LLC
LaVergne TN
LVHW010305070426
835508LV00026B/3437